First published by David Abbott 201.

Copyright
© David Abbott, 2016

The moral right of David Abbott to be identified as the Author of this work has been asserted by him in accordance with the Copyright, Designs and Patents Act 1988

Dedication

Huge thanks go to two people without whom this book would not have been written - Chris Davidson for his invaluable advice and guidance on writing my first book, and my wonderful wife, Annette, for all the endless copy checking and editing.

I also want to thank my Butterpillar friends for getting me here - Fred, Anthony, Liz, Jayne and Jay, you've been brilliant support.

Contents

Introduction

Perhaps you are one of the lucky few who have no difficulty working out what is the best price you can charge for your product or service, you always succeed in charging it, and you are totally confident no one else could possibly get a higher price.

Most businesses aren't like that.

When it comes to pricing, there's always the fear that charging that little bit extra will lose the sale entirely, so it feels safer just to knock a bit off. Much better to get the sale, right?

There is always pressure to move prices down. What about going in the other direction? Most companies either don't review their prices unless they absolutely have to, or they stick to a price until a cost increase forces them to do something about it.

What kind of a difference would it make if you could successfully increase your prices?

If your business typically makes around 10% net profit, what difference would a 2%, 3% or 4% increase in your average prices make for you? Well, because your costs have not changed, all the extra income from those price increases goes straight to your bottom line. Your net profit improves to around 12%, 13% or 14%. To put it another way, if you make 10% net profit and you can grow your prices by 4%, you have increased your profit by 40%!

Does 4% sound too challenging?

Back in 1997, the average price for a typical cup of coffee was around 50p and it was quite a simple product. You walked into a shop, watched hot water being poured onto instant granules, added cream, milk, or sugar if that was to your taste, and walked out. Extremely simple. In 1998, the price of a cup of coffee suddenly got a lot higher when Starbucks opened in the UK. Now the average price was closer to £2.50. You weren't buying coffee anymore - you were buying a coffee experience. You weren't buying it from a shop assistant, but a barista. You had to wait while machines gurgled, hissed and spluttered. The language changed; it was no longer small, medium, or large, but grande, venti, or trenta.

It is still just a cup of coffee, but now it's 5 times more expensive. Have the cost of raw ingredients increased 5 times? No. The equipment is more expensive than a simple kettle, but the cost of the equipment amounts to pence when spread over the thousands of coffees it makes.

So, if Starbucks can increase coffee prices by 5 times (a 400% increase!), can you achieve a 5% increase? What about a 10% increase? Would that make a difference to your business?

If this sounds like an exciting prospect then this book is for you.

How to Use This Book

This book is split into 5 parts.

You can work through the book, one section at a time, to do a full pricing analysis on your business.

Alternatively, perhaps all you want are some ideas on how to price a new product you are about to launch. In that case you can dip into the relevant sections, explore the ideas and concepts, and get some ideas you can put into practice.

The book is deliberately short. Long technical books on pricing might get used during a university course, but very few businesses will have time to wade through such a weighty tome; instead, this has been written to allow you to read it cover to cover in a couple of hours. That means you are much more likely to get some real value out of the ideas presented here.

Section one - why pricing is difficult

We explore what it is about pricing that makes it one of the harder things for businesses to get right.

Section two - analysing pricing options

This is an important step which will allow you to work out the highest price you can reasonably charge for something.

This section involves some analysis of the business, so that you understand what your true profitability is. You identify the potential range of prices you could possibly charge in the market place. Not all purchases are the same (you don't treat buying a bar of chocolate the same way you would treat buying a house), so you understand the mode of buying your customers are in.

Although section two delivers important answers to the question "what's the highest price I can charge", if time is short you can skip part two and go straight into part three - "how do I promote a higher price?"

Section three - introducing the pricing concepts

Part three is all about how your customer makes decisions on what is a reasonable price to pay.

This section therefore focuses on how we **communicate the price** in a way that helps the customer make a decision to buy at that price.

The basis of this section is this - we're all human. We would like to think that we are purely logical, that when we have a decision in front of us we apply the reasoning part of our brain and make a logical and rational decision about whether a particular price is fair or not. In fact, the vast majority of the decisions we take in any day are driven by our subconscious, the automatic part of our brain, and we use the logical part of our brain to rationalise those decisions.

So part three looks at eight psychological factors that come into play and how, by understanding those different pricing concepts, you can find a way to communicate a higher price that the customer is prepared to pay.

Section four - choosing the right pricing concepts to apply

In section three we explored eight different pricing concepts. A business would be mad to try to apply all eight at the same time. You would confuse yourself horribly, you would probably confuse your customers dreadfully, and you would have no idea which concept was working.

In section four you decide which of the different pricing concepts you're going to apply, how you're going to apply them, what impact you think they might have, and how you cope with that impact.

Section five - making sure it's working

You need to make sure that whatever you try is actually making a difference; this section is about how to measure that impact. Measurement means you can do more of what's working or try something different if the ideas are not working.

Section 1 - Introduction

Chapter 1. Why a Platypus?

Imagine you suddenly become the owner of a platypus - a living, breathing, 2-year-old, cuddly, friendly little platypus. You keep it for a few months, you love it and care for it, but then for one reason or another you decide you can't keep it anymore. Perhaps you can't keep it healthy, and you need to sell it. What do you charge for a real live platypus? What would the price be?

You can't use Google. If you do try to find the price of a real, live platypus on Google you will find it is extremely difficult. You may find one or two people interested in buying one, but you can't find anybody selling one so you can't establish a market price.

So where do you start?

Most businesses have this kind of situation. They have a product or service where they are struggling to identify the optimum price. It is, of course, a little easier for a business because they will have competition, so other products and services are available for them to measure themselves against. But is that the best price to charge? Is that the highest price that could be charged? They are assuming that the competitor has already worked out the maximum price.

Generally, they don't know. So our platypus is a metaphor for all the pricing problems businesses face.

Chapter 2. The 4 Ps of Marketing

Many people will have heard of the four P's of marketing: product, place, promotion, and price.

They are a memory aid for business to make sure that when they are planning their marketing, they consider the main elements for what constitutes a marketing plan. There are many other things to take into consideration, but this is just a simple way to remind oneself in business that these factors need to be thought through.

Product. Most companies are usually clear about what it is they're offering. You know what your product or service is, you will normally understand what the demand for that product or service is, and you are clear about what it is you are taking to market.

Place. Given the product, an organisation is generally clear about their channel to market, the route through which you're bringing your product or service to market. If you're selling cans of beans, you know that you're probably going to be selling partly through online sales, but mostly through supermarkets and convenience stores.

Promotion. This is the mix of communication activities that you employ to tell everybody about your product and why yours is better than the competition. Advertising, press releases, exhibitions, merchandise at stores, offers such as two-for-ones, direct mail, social media and more. It's the variety of things that you employ to try and promote your product ahead of the competition.

This is a little bit harder because you have a wide range of choices for what you might do to promote the product, and it's not always absolutely clear which are the best ones to apply. However, there are countless marketing books all focused on how to promote your product effectively.

Pricing. This is a little bit different and is often the hardest thing to get right.

There are some easy steps you can take with pricing, such as cost plus pricing or simply matching the competition, but because they're easy and are used by everybody they are not necessarily the optimum way to price.

Are you really charging the best price that you can? It's often where you experience the most anguish. The worry is that if you try to charge the price you would like to, you will lose sales. Nobody likes to lose sales, so there is always the tendency to try to push the price a little bit lower, just to be sure that you close the deal.

Companies with a sales force also have an issue. Whenever a sales person meets a buyer they will typically end up talking about price, sometimes for the majority of the meeting. That's for a number of reasons. One is because the buyers are trained to talk about prices and are generally incentivised to get a lower price. It's also because of a psychological factor where the easiest thing you can bring to mind (price!) is the first thing you focus on. This will therefore be the topic of conversation. The consequence of all this is the sales team often comes back to the organisation and say "We could have sold more if our prices had been a little bit lower."

All of this means that most organisations price their products or services too low, and they struggle to know what they could actually charge.

But there are really only two parts to pricing; one is to analyse the situation to establish what you could be charging, and the other is the best way to communicate that price to the potential customer. And that's it.

Chapter 3. Fermi Problems

Enrico Fermi was an Italian physicist who lived from 1901 to 1954. He created the world's first nuclear reactor, and built it under the viewing stand of one of Chicago University's football fields - no health and safety in those days!

One of the things he worked on was the Manhattan Project, helping the USA develop its first nuclear bomb. He witnessed the nuclear detonation tests in the Jornada del Muerto desert about 35 miles southeast of Socorro, New Mexico. He famously estimated the yield of the explosion by dropping pieces of paper from his hand during the blast; he knew how far away the explosion was, how high his hand was above the ground, and he could see how far the blast displaced the falling paper. He did some maths in his head and got very close to the actual yield.

Ever since then there have been a class of problems described as 'Fermi Problems'.

Let's illustrate this with an example. Find a piece of paper and write down how many piano tuners you think work in London.

Ready?

How would Fermi have approached this?

Let's start by guessing how many people live in London (my guess is 10m). How many people live in an average house (let's say 4), so that's 2.5m homes in London. How many homes have a piano? My guess is one in one hundred, so that's 25,000 pianos.

Next, how long does it take to tune a piano? My estimate is about 2h including the time to drive between customers, so that's about 4 pianos tuned per day per piano tuner. There are 365 days in the year, but subtracting weekends (104 days) and another 31 days for holidays leaves 230 working days. So doing 4 pianos per day means each piano tuner can tune 920 pianos per year.

If there are 25,000 pianos and each tuner does 920 of them then there are 27 full time piano tuners in London.

How close is this to your guess? If your guess is quite different to 27, which number would you trust more - your complete guess or the 27 that we've just worked out?

The point about this is that we don't actually know if there really are 27 piano tuners in London, but if we want to estimate that number we're much more likely to get close to it by making a series of reasonable assumptions and doing the maths, rather than by just guessing outright. Each of our estimates is probably wrong, but with luck they won't be too far out, and because some estimates will be too high and some too low the errors should cancel out.

In Section 2 - Analysis we are going to use some tools which make a series of estimates about your business. You are going to be treating these questions as if they are 'Fermi Problems'. Hopefully you will now be convinced that by following these processes you will end up with some insights into your business which will be close to the truth and which will be better than a simple gut feeling or guess.

Section 2 - Analysis

There are four elements to the analysis stage. Let's quickly summarise each...

1. Simplified ABC (Activity-based Costing).

This establishes the true profitability of a product, product group, market segment, channel or however else you segment your market or your business.

2. Buyer Influences and Value Perception

What are the things that motivate a buyer to choose a particular product versus another? These are also known as Critical Sales Factors (CSFs). They are the various elements a buyer is consciously or unconsciously weighing when they make a decision to buy product A versus product B. These CSFs are also used to measure the value the customer gets from each product.

3. Buyer Behaviour

Not all buyer decisions are the same. If the buyer is considering a low-cost, high-frequency commodity item or a high-cost, low-frequency strategic item, the buying mode, or the mental processes they go through are different. This means that different types of pricing decisions are being made.

4. Price Potential

There is seldom only one possible price for a product or service - things like quality, features, options, convenience, scarcity, and how prices are presented all affect the final price. This means there is a range of possible prices for the product we are selling. These range from the maximum price that could possibly be charged, down to the lowest credible price that could be charged, and we then decide where within those possible prices we want to position ourselves.

Full activity-based costing is quite a complicated area, so we're going to simplify it. At the end of this you will have a much clearer idea of where your profit is coming from and what your pricing options are.

Activity-based costing is sharing each cost involved in producing, marketing and selling something proportional to the activity or effort in each of those areas. The point of it is to measure true profitability, and this is probably best explained with an example.

Back in the 1990's, a company in the U.K. called Microvitec manufactured monitors. In those days a computer monitor was one of the old bulky TV-shaped displays.

This particular company had two main markets.

One market was called process control. A process control machine is a computer-controlled piece of equipment sitting on a factory floor making something. Because the equipment is computer-controlled you need a display of some kind in order to interact with the machine, and these displays are built into the device.

The second market was called financial. These are the city traders, with their braces, checking what's happening to currency and stock markets on multiple screens, comparing lots of financial data, and making decisions on whether they are going to buy or sell.

		(000s)
Process Control	Sales	£15,000
	GM%	45%
	GM	£6,750
Financial	Sales	£15,000
	GM%	28%
	GM	£4,200
Total	Sales	£30,000
	GM%	37%
	GM	£10,950
Overheads	Wages	£4,500
	Rent/Rates	£600
	Utilities	£600
	Marketing	£500
	R&D	£1,000
	Admin	£300
	Bank	£150
	Other	£200
Total		£7,850
Operating Profit		£3,100
OP%		10%

Microvitec turned over £30 million. Each of the two markets was roughly £15 million. But the financial market had an average gross margin (the difference between sales income and the cost of the raw materials to make the products) around 28%, whereas for process control the gross margin was 45%.

As a result, process control was a lot more popular within the business. It had much more focus, and more resources, all on the basis that the product sector was more profitable.

Let's look at the company as a whole. When you add the sales from the two sectors together, add the cost of materials together, and subtract the total material costs from the total sales costs the gross margin was £11 million - about 37%. From this you subtract overheads such as wages, R&D and marketing which add up to just less than £8 million, leaving £3 million profit, which is approximately 10%.

A different story starts to emerge when we start to dig down into the detail of the activities taking place in each of the areas, and what that means in terms of how costs should be fairly shared out.

In the process control part of the company there is a lot of variety. There were 108 different products and they were sold to 108 different customers, because each customer manufactured its own unique computer-aided machine. As a result, each monitor must be unique to fit into and interface with the machine. For 108 customers there are therefore 108 different models going down the production line, each in relatively low quantities, resulting in 108 different batch changeovers, 108 different test jigs, and 108 different bills of material that need to be maintained internally by the team. Because there are 108 customers, there are 4 salespeople. The development time for each product is relatively short because each product is a close variant of another product - the company took a product for one customer and adapted it for another customer, therefore development times were around 6 months.

The finance product range is entirely different. Fewer models go through production, but they do so in very high volumes. There are only 20 key customers with a single salesperson managing them because most of the customers are all in the square mile of London. The models have an 18-month development time because each is an almost completely new design.

Process Control	Financial
108 models	4 models
4 sales people	1 sales person
108 customers	20 key customers
6 month development	18 month replacement
Low volumes on line	High volumes on line

The next step for these two markets is to start to apportion the costs appropriate to the amount of effort that takes place, or in other words, the number of activities.

Let's start with the department that manufactures test jigs. The wage cost for that department should be split depending upon how many test jigs are made. In the financial marketplace, they make one or two test jigs per year because there is an 18-month replacement schedule over four models. For the process control marketplace, the department made about 50 test jigs per year because there are 108 customers with a 6-month development time.

In procurement, it takes the same amount of effort to place a purchase order for 100 items as it does to place one for 10,000 items - only the number on the page changes. However, more purchase orders are required for 108 different models compared to 4 different models.

Manufacturing like to make lots of the same product. It takes time to change a production line over or retool from one product to another, with a cost involved every time that changeover happens. Low volumes with multiple line changeovers are more expensive.

Even marketing has different levels of activity for each of the market sectors. Process control is not a single homogenous segment - there are customers manufacturing production equipment for a vast range of industries, so marketing effort is spread across many different communication channels. On the other hand, the financial marketplace is much more compact and easier to reach.

The next step, once you have worked out what drives activity and therefore cost, is to use a count of those activities per product sector to apportion costs. In other words, apportion the wage costs per department, then the various cost centres such as marketing, R&D, admin.

		(000s)	P Control (000s)	Financial (000s)
Process Control	Sales	£15,000	£15,000	
	GM%	45%	45%	
	GM	£6,750	£6,750	
Financial	Sales	£15,000		£15,000
	GM%	28%		28%
	GM	£4,200		£4,200
Total	Sales	£30,000	£15,000	£15,000
	GM%	37%	45%	28%
	GM	£10,950	£6,750	£4,200
Overheads	Wages	£4,500	£3,607	£893
	Rent/Rates	£600	£300	£300
	Utilities	£600	£300	£300
	Marketing	£500	£400	£100
	R&D	£1,000	£800	£200
	Admin	£300	£195	£105
	Bank	£150	£75	£75
	Other	£200	£100	£100
Total		£7,850	£5,777	£2,073
Operating Profit		£3,100	£973	£2,127
OP%		10%	6%	14%

When this was done for Microvitec, although we started off with a £15 million turnover for process control with a 45% gross margin, the much higher costs mean that there is a net profit of just under £1 million.

Doing the same thing with the financial marketplace gives us a completely different picture. Subtracting the costs leaves us with £2.1 million net profit.

So the *real* profitability for the financial marketplace is 14% net profit, and the process control marketplace 6% net profit.

Prior to this analysis, the darling of the organisation was process control, because a 45% gross margin looked incredibly attractive. But by the time we actually apply the costs where they are incurred instead of simply sharing them across the business, it's clear that more focus should go into the financial marketplace.

When you believe you have 45% of margin to play with, there is a danger that you will be tempted into inappropriate discounts. Perhaps you are in discussions with a prospect which looks attractive but the competition is after the same customer, and you decide to offer them a 15% discount to get the business. After all, that's still 30% gross margin. Except now that particular customer is being sold to at a loss!

Chapter 5. Buyer Influences and Value Perception

Although price is one of the factors that probably (but not always) is a factor influencing whether you make a sale, it is not the only factor. This chapter explores what else influences the success of the sale, and how those factors map to your customer's value expectations.

It is very easy to end up focusing on the price at which you are selling your product or service. If you are negotiating face-to-face then price will inevitably be one of the main points of discussion. If your customers buy your products from a channel where no negotiation takes place, such as from a website or a retailer, you still think long and hard about the end-user price you can charge.

Because of this, it is easy to end up thinking that price is not only the most important factor influencing the sale, sometimes it might seem like it is the **only** factor.

In actual fact, there are many factors which will influence why a customer might buy something.

For example, quality might be a key issue; or availability; or whether it is made in the UK. Perhaps the ability to rapidly supply the item (in other words, very short lead-times), the colour and style of the product, the specification or some level of exclusivity might be key.

There are many factors that come into play, even with really unusual products. Let's imagine you have a venue for weddings. If it is a particularly unusual venue, which makes it different and exciting, then it would make no sense whatsoever to price match and compare oneself against a standard hotel venue. After all, put yourself in the shoes of the customer - a wedding is a special occasion for everyone, it's the most important event in their child's life. They are looking for something to bring the whole event to life and make it an incredible, memorable day for all those involved. All these factors influence both the propensity to buy and the price they are prepared to pay. If you don't take those factors into account, you risk getting your pricing wrong.

A list of factors could include:

- Cost (obviously!)
- Specification
- Availability
- Speed of supply
- Quality
- Reliability
- Length of the supply chain
- Exclusivity
- How exciting it is
- How useful it is
- Whether you are prepared to hold buffer stock
- Trade/credit terms
- Colour
- Style
- Whether it is made in the UK
- Brand recognition
- Unique features/benefits
- Green or fair trade
- Sustainability
- Ethical position of the manufacturer

These are the Critical Sales Factors (CSFs) which influence whether your customer buys from you or your competitor.

The first step in the process we are going to go through will be to list the specific factors which influence your customer's purchasing decision.

Before we do, though, there is a useful additional concept to understand. Knowing what is genuinely motivating the buyer will help you to be certain that you are not ignoring an important factor which is leading your customer to make one buying decision rather than another. We want to understand the customer's genuine **needs** and **benefits**.

Let's start with an illustration to explain this.

There is a classic example used in marketing which goes like this: nobody wants to buy a quarter-inch drill bit, what they really want is a quarter-inch hole in the wall. The point being made in the example is that the customer doesn't really care about the drill bit, what they care about is the result. The 'feature' or 'specification' is that the drill bit is one quarter inches in diameter; the 'benefit' is the quarter inch hole it makes in a wall.

This can be taken a step further. In reality, nobody really wants a quarter-inch hole in the wall either. What they really want is to hang a nice picture or to put up a shelf to improve storage. So the real, genuine underlying benefit the customer is trying to get is a beautiful room or more space. The quarter-inch drill bit is just the tangible item they are buying to get their final benefit or outcome.

One of the most important factors for your customer might be quality. But what does that really mean? What is the benefit, to them, of quality? It might be to take risk out of the purchase, and if the person you deal with is a buyer it could mean job security. For a company owner it might mean keeping a production line going because down time is incredibly expensive.

As a final illustration, think about buying a car. Some manufacturers sell almost the same car under different brands; you can buy a VW Passat for one price or an Audi A6 at a higher price, and largely, underneath the skin, they will be identical cars, with identical fixtures, seats, engines, suspension, etc. But the Audi might carry a 30% price premium. There are some quality variations but the big one is brand difference. And what's driving (no pun intended!) the issue? There are a number of psychological factors around what the car says about you, how you feel when you're driving it, how proud it makes you feel, and many other factors.

We'll go through the process step by step, starting with the following table:

Critical Sales Factor	Benefit	Benefit	Benefit
FROZEN	Fresh Taste	No waste	Long shelf life
CONVENIENT	Portion control	Easy to use	flexible, works around you
HEALTY	Healthy eating	low fat/sugar/salt	Guilt free
FREE FROM	Suitable to allergy	doesn't excite	No compromise
AUTHENTIC	Great taste	Great product Availability	Reveals recipe.
Home Delivery	Saves time/money		

Step 1

For each of your products (or product groups), list the main factors that influence the customer's purchasing decision.

Critical Sales Factor	Benefit	Benefit	Benefit
Specification			
Quality			
30 day terms			
Price			

Step 2

For each factor, explore the benefit for the customer, including what the psychological motivation might be. Then think about what **that** then means in terms of benefit; and if needs be, what **that** also means. Go as deep as you have to. In this example we have only explored two levels of underlying benefit.

Critical Sales Factor	Benefit	Benefit	Benefit
Specification	Works with their manufacturing equipment	No need to retool or redesign manufacturing line	
Quality	Reliability	Production line doesn't stop which would cost money	
30 day terms	Helps their cashflow		
Price	Helps their profitability		

Looking at what quality really means to the customer, it must be the case that there is really an additional CSF that hasn't been considered - if the line can stop because of quality problems, it can also stop because of supply problems. Product availability must also be important. So the real list of CSFs should be:

Critical Sales Factor	Benefit	Benefit	Benefit
Specification	Works with their manufacturing equipment	No need to retool or redesign manufacturing line	
Quality	Reliability	Production line doesn't stop which would cost money	
30 day terms	Helps their cashflow		
Price	Helps their profitability		
Availability	Production line doesn't stop which would cost money		

Before we move onto the next step, this is also an opportunity to consider the basic needs that are being addressed, or the most basic benefits that are being enjoyed. Does this give you any clues regarding alternative solutions that might work for your customer?

Let's use the quarter-inch drill bit example again. Assume that a quarter-inch drill bit costs £0.40. But the fundamental needs of the customer are a beautiful room with a gorgeous picture; they are not excited about owning a quarter-inch drill bit. In fact, they have to also own a drill, be confident about drilling into walls, they have to tidy up the mess, and they have to worry about things not being level or falling off the wall.

Now imagine that someone invents a special gizmo which cleverly attaches itself to the wall, so no hook is needed! Maybe it costs £3.50. You might imagine that something costing almost nine times as much and which looks completely different to the drill bit you are selling is not a competing product, and that your only competitors are other drill bit manufacturers, but that's not the case.

So as part of this step, look at the different needs you have identified and think about direct competitors, indirect competitors (do the same job a slightly different way), and substitutes (achieve the ultimate need a completely different way).

We'll use this information in step 4.

Step 3

Now that we have our list of CSFs, we're going to work out how important each one is. It is very unlikely that every CSF is of equal importance.

We have 5 CSFs for our products: specification, quality, 30 day terms, price and availability. We have to use a judgement call to estimate the score each would get out of 10, if your customers were going to score them (of course, you can also go to each of your customers and actually ask them; do be careful, though, what people say is not always the same as what they do, and it is what they do that counts).

Critical Sales Factor	Weighting
Specification	
Quality	
30 day terms	
Price	
Availability	
Total	

Step 4

Now, you write down how well each of your products scores for each of the CSFs. Multiply the score times the weighting for each of the CSFs, and add them together to get a total 'value' for each product.

Critical Sales Factor	Weighting	Product 1		Product 2		Product 3	
		Score	Total	Score	Total	Score	Total
Specification	9	8	72	10	90	10	90
Quality	10	6	60	8	80	10	100
30 day terms	4	10	40	10	40	10	40
Price	6	6	36	5	30	3	18
Availability	10	9	90	10	100	6	60
Total			298		340		308

What this allows you to do is compare your alternative products against each other; many companies will have a "good, better, best" offering in a particular segment. You will see what the increments in value are that you're providing with each step up in the product performance.

Importantly, you can add additional product score/total columns for your competitor's products, and compare the value you provide against the competition. Even more importantly, you can include the indirect competitors and complete substitutes to look at the amount your customers are really prepared to pay for a solution to their needs.

This gives you some information about where you might be able to competitively price your products.

If you are providing more value than the competition you can consider raising your prices (and because price is one of the CSFs in this example, when you do, the value will decrease until it is in line with the competition).

If you have a range of products, you can compare the value provided by each to ensure there is a clearly different value proposition for each.

Perhaps there are simple changes you can make to some of the CSFs - for example, if availability is really important to the customer, it might be easy and cost little to provide a week's worth of buffer stock. You can assess out how that change will improve the value you provide to the customer, and therefore potentially the price you can charge.

One of the interesting things with the example above is that we have included price as part of the overall calculation of value. There is no right or wrong way here. You can repeat the exercise but take price out of the list of CSFs, because that then allows you to map the value provided by the other

CSFs against price - see the table and chart below. In this example the price is not expressed as a score but is shown as the actual price.

Critical Sales Factor	Weighting	Product 1		Product 2		Product 3	
		Score	Total	Score	Total	Score	Total
Specification	9	8	72	10	90	10	90
Quality	10	6	60	8	80	10	100
30 day terms	4	10	40	10	40	10	40
Availability	10	9	90	10	100	6	60
Total			262		310		290
Price			£230		£250		£350

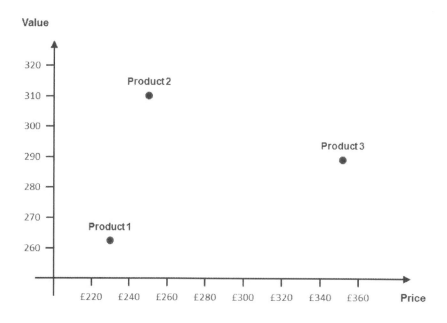

Each method has advantages and disadvantages. Try them both.

There is a final thing to consider before we move on. Not all sales are simple direct negotiations with the final consumer. Sometimes more than one person is involved in the buying decision, in which case you need to think about the motivating factors for each; and sometimes the person or organisation you sell to is not the final consumer of the product, so it might help to think about the motivating factors for each link in the chain between you and the end consumer.

Chapter 6. Buyer Behaviour

Buyers don't treat all buying decisions the same. This chapter explores how we act depending upon the circumstances of the purchase, and what that means to pricing decisions.

Not all purchases are the same.

Different purchases involve different amounts of consideration and mental effort. As consumers, we don't deliberate as much when buying a bar of chocolate as we do when purchasing a gym membership or holiday.

The same is also true for business purchases. The equivalent level of buyer effort does not go into purchasing copier paper as it does into buying new machinery for the shop floor.

One way to map the different modes of buyer behaviour is to compare the frequency of purchase against the importance of the purchase.

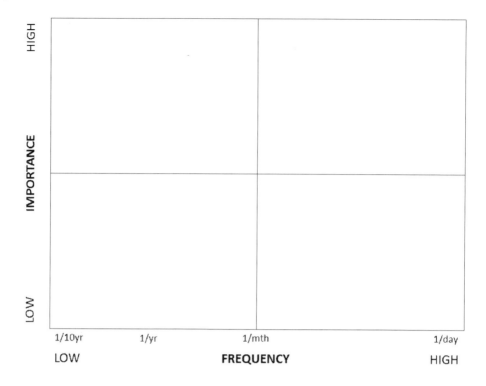

A high frequency of purchase might be once a day, while a low frequency could be once every 10 years.

'Importance' is somewhat intangible or subjective. It is a measure of the impact if your customers get a purchase wrong; what the effect will be if they do not choose the right solution; or how much time and effort they put into the purchasing decision. To a certain extent 'Importance' is also a measure of how expensive the item is, as the more they spend on something, the more seriously they treat the purchase.

The next step is to add the various items your customer buys. Let's start with an example of a consumer.

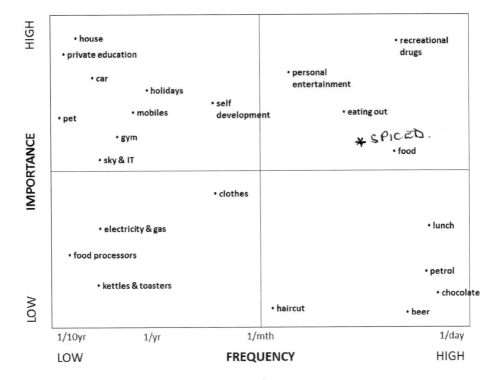

High frequency, low importance: examples are lunch, beer, a bar of chocolate, a haircut (though for some a haircut is a more frequent and important purchase than for others).

Low frequency, low importance: for instance, electricity and gas, a food processor, kettles, toaster, perhaps clothes - although clothes, like haircuts, will vary between people who don't care what they wear and those that like fashion.

High frequency, high importance: such as personal entertainment, food, eating out at nice restaurants, or season tickets for your favourite football club.

Low frequency, high importance: which could include buying a house, a private education for your child, buying a car, taking a holiday, or buying your mobile phone on an 18-month to 2-year contract.

Let's consider clothing in more detail. This is where segmentation and understanding the buyer motivation makes a big difference. For some people, buying clothes is a simple transaction - it is relatively low frequency and is of low importance to them, they don't enjoy shopping for things to wear. They have no interest in fashion, they simply want functional clothes so they can get on with the rest of their life. Other people place a great deal of importance on looking good, they enjoy shopping for clothes, and enjoy wearing the latest fashion - for them, frequency and importance will both be higher.

Colours matter, the style matters, making a statement, quality, brand, the badge all matter. Given two identical T-shirts, with one having a strong brand or logo, they would buy the branded one and pay more for it.

Taken even further, tailor-made outfits will probably be high importance but also low frequency. They tend to be expensive, you can't easily take them back if you are not satisfied so they have to be right, and (for men) you probably don't buy 15 tailor-made suits per year.

These differences for different buyer segments are true for haircuts and almost everything else on the chart. Different segments of your market will transact with different frequencies and place different levels of importance depending upon what motivates them. It is therefore possible that you will have slightly different maps of buyer behaviour depending upon the different segments your products address and the different buyer motivations in each segment.

Given the map of buyer behaviour, the four quadrants can be broadly categorised as:

- High frequency, low importance: **consumables**
- Low frequency, low importance: **enablers**
- High frequency, high importance: **self-fulfilment**
- Low frequency, high importance: **lifestyle**

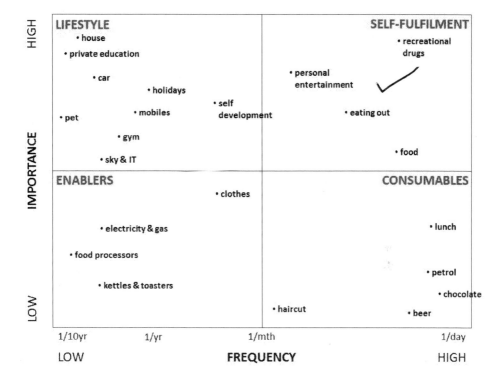

The principles are very similar for business purchases. In that situation the chart may well look like:

High

• assets/plant
• ERP s/w

  • servers   • marketing

• key components

• minor plant

• health & safety

• telephony/ISP • finance/factoring   • temp labour

• HR

• insurance

• accountants   • recruitment   • minor components

IMPORTANCE

• utilities • laptops/software

• furniture

• catering

• travel

• cleaners

• petrol

Low

• copy paper • coffee/tea   • nuts & bolts

1/10yr   1/yr   1/mth   1/day

LOW   **FREQUENCY**   HIGH

<u>High frequency</u>, <u>low importance</u>: such as petrol, nuts, bolts, resistors, transistors, copier paper, or coffee and tea for the office - simple and low-cost items, large volume components for manufacturing, perhaps things that are so low cost you don't even count them, you just replenish the bins when they get close to empty.

<u>Low frequency</u>, <u>low importance</u>: examples include the furniture, the desks and chairs, catering contracts, laptops and PCs; important business tools but ones where, if they go wrong, you can easily replace them; they are the basic things that allow you to operate a business.

Things get a little more interesting for the two 'high importance' quadrants.

High frequency, high importance: these could include key components in your product (for example, if you happen to manufacture iPhones, then the display is probably a key component), health and safety equipment, temporary labour; things you are consuming a lot of but have a big impact if they go wrong or if you can't get them, there might be few or no substitutes, and they have to be high quality.

Low frequency, high importance: for instance, ERP planning software that runs the business, your accountants, insurance, HR, or the marketing agency you work with because you don't change it every month and you want an agency that is going to drive the business forward and help you to succeed; you don't want to lose both money and market share because you're not marketing yourself effectively.

Again, the four quadrants can be broadly categorised as:

- High frequency, low importance: **consumables**
- Low frequency, low importance: **enablers**
- High frequency, high importance: **production**
- Low frequency, high importance: **strategic**

You have now developed your map of buyer behaviour for the segment that your product or service addresses. We will use this later when we go through the different pricing concepts as different concepts apply to different buyer behaviour situation. This will therefore help to guide you in terms of which are the most appropriate concepts you might want to try.

Chapter 7. Price Potential

In any market there is a range of permissible prices. This chapter works out what that range is, from the lowest reasonable price to the highest acceptable price.

For any market segment there is a range of permissible prices, from the lowest price you can charge to the highest. There is also a minimum price which is still profitable, and hopefully this is lower than the lowest price being charged.

Maximum Price

Let's start at the top and work down.

For any particular product in any particular segment, there will normally be a reasonable maximum that you might be able to charge. But you have to be cautious about your assumptions regarding that maximum price. Back in

1997, given that a typical price for a cup of coffee bought on the high street was around £0.50, people might have concluded that a maximum price might be about £1.00; until Starbucks entered the market and completely broke the comparisons that existed, selling coffee for around £2.50.

Despite Starbucks' success, there must still be a maximum at which sales drop off to a negligible level. You would probably struggle to achieve volume sales if your coffee was priced at £20 per cup!

For any particular segment, you need to consider the factors that are influencing what people are prepared to buy and to work out what a potential maximum might be. To do this you use the output from Chapter 5. Buyer Influences and Value Perception. In completing that chapter you will have done four things:

a. Worked out what the fundamental motivating factors are (or what fundamental benefits are being sought).
b. Worked out what alternatives could also satisfy those motivating factors or satisfy those needs.
c. Worked out how well you are delivering value against those needs.
d. Compared that value with what the competition is doing.

That means you already know the highest price anyone is charging in this segment, and you know whether there is additional value that can be charged for. And that's going to give you an understanding of what a reasonable maximum price could be.

Lowest Credible Price

Next, there is the lowest credible price.

Occasionally, you might see a well-known brand being sold for a remarkably low price; most people would be extremely pleased and would buy at that price, but they know it is a short-term promotion. If the price stays at that level it damages the brand.

More fundamentally, if a product or service is offered at an extremely low price, then it communicates something about the quality you should expect. If you try to launch a new brand of chocolate and you price a bar of that chocolate at a penny, there would be some people who would try it, but a lot of people would conclude you were using inferior ingredients and it's either going to taste horrible or it's going to damage your health.

The same is true for cars. For a new car brand, there is probably a price that is too cheap, because it will be expected to be unreliable and unrewarding to drive.

With clothing, if the item is too cheap, the expectation will be that it will fall apart after one wear; unless you're in the market for disposable clothes that is going to disappoint the customers.

To establish the lowest credible price you should research all the competitors that currently exist, but you also need to use the same work regarding benefits and Critical Sales Factors to understand where the psychological tipping point will be at which the customer turns around and says "there is something wrong here, this is too cheap".

You now have a band of prices where you are trying to move from the bottom towards the top.

Break-Even Price

There is also a break-even point for your product. This was arrived at in Chapter 4. Simplified ABC; hopefully that break-even price is below the lowest credible price. Sometimes the break-even price is higher than the lowest credible price, and that means that anybody selling at the bottom of this band is selling at a loss.

Some organisations deliberately try to occupy the lowest price point in a market. The value airlines, such as Ryanair, are obvious examples. However, they are very smart about their approach,. They absolutely understand their true margins for everything, using Simplified ABC or something similar, and they know when they are making money; they are ruthless at driving costs out of their operation to move the break-even price as low as possible; and they move many items out of the base product into options, such as baggage allowances, priority boarding, and food or drink.

Another circumstance, mentioned already, where an organisation might decide to sell at or below the break-even price is for promotional purposes, either as a short-term offer or used strategically on certain products as loss-leaders to drive sales of more profitable products.

In general there are very few companies in any market that can successfully follow a low-cost/low-price model and make it work. More often what happens is that competitors follow anyone that decreases their price, there is a race to the bottom, and some companies go out of business.

Putting It Together

Now that the different price bands for your market segment have been identified you can plot where your price is relative to those bands. Very simply, you now have the tools to decide where you have room to increase a price, and by how much you could potentially increase it.

Having decided what your new price is going to be, you need to communicate it. You need to market the price in such a way that it is accepted. And that's the subject of the next section.

Section 3 - Pricing Concepts

We know, from the previous section, that there is no single absolute price for anything, there are usually a range of allowable prices. We know that factors such as underlying benefits influence a customer's motivation. We know that the way a customer approaches a purchase depends on a balance between how frequently an item is bought compared to its importance. All of this means that different psychological factors come into play when a customer decides if a price for something is a fair price to pay.

In this section we are going to explore eight different psychological concepts that influence a pricing decision.

Chapter 8. Price Relativity

Everybody compares the price they're going to pay with something. Often it is a competing product, but it could also be another thing they'd like to spend their money on. If customers are going to make that comparison then guide the comparison by providing alternative prices, which can include decoy prices.

Some years ago The Economist was advertising for new subscribers. They offered the online version for $59, the print version for $125, and both together - also for $125.

SUBSCRIPTIONS

OPINION
WORLD
BUSINESS
FINANCE & ECONOMICS
SCIENCE & TECHNOLOGY
PEOPLE
BOOKS & ARTS
MARKETS & DATA
DIVERSIONS

Welcome to

The Economist Subscription Centre

Pick the type of subscription you want to buy or renew.

☐ **Economist.com subscription** - US $59.00
One-year subscription to Economist.com.
Includes online access to all articles from
The Economist since 1997.

☐ **Print subscription** - US $125.00
One-year subscription to the print edition
of *The Economist*.

☐ **Print & web subscription** - US $125.00
One-year subscription to the print edition
of *The Economist* and online access to all
articles from *The Economist* since 1997.

To a lot of people it looked like a mistake had been made by The Economist. After all, when you bundle two items together you usually add the two prices together and then take a little bit off. In this case, the sum of the prices is $184, so you would expect the bundle price to be $179 or $169.

The Economist was being very clever. If you ask people which they would buy, the online version only or the print plus online version for twice the price (which is what The Economist want to sell), the majority go for the cheaper option. You can imagine their thinking... "well, for an extra $66, I can go and have a nice meal out, I could spend that on a second subscription to something else, and do I want all that paper cluttering the house anyway?".

But when you introduce the print-only version, also at $125, what happens is that the majority don't decide to buy the cheaper internet only option anymore; the majority instead choose the print plus internet option - because it looks like a bargain[1]. Because the print only option is $125 and print plus internet is also $125, it looks like staff at The Economist have made a mistake. The thinking is now "let's subscribe quickly before they realise". No one actually chooses the print only option, but just the fact that it was there makes the print plus internet look like a bargain.

Look at it this way. The Economist has two ways to deliver its content, either online or in print. If the two options were put on a graph of price vs value it might look like this:

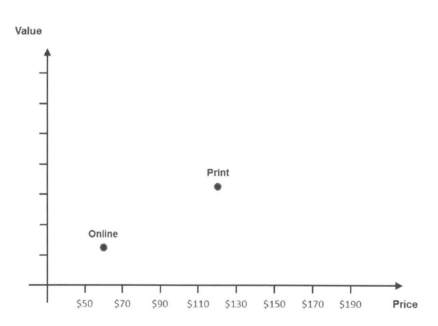

The Economist has the option to create a third product by combining the first two. In doing so, you would normally expect the value to the customer to increase, and the price to increase, like this:

[1] Predictably Irrational: The Hidden Forces That Shape Our Decisions - Dan Ariely

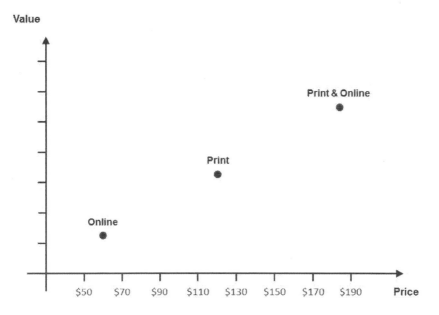

However, what the Economist did was price the combined bundle the same as the print only version. Their customers now have two products at an identical price but different levels of value:

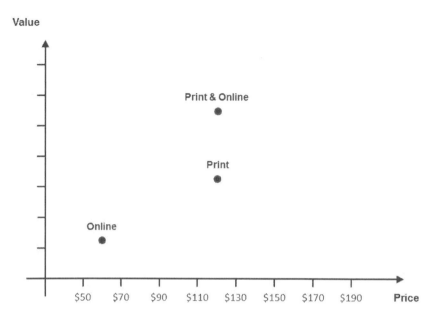

When a customer is presented with a price an internal comparison takes place. The comparison is between competing products, alternative solutions or simply other things the money can be spent on. Given that customers are going to make that comparison, what The Economist has done is to guide that comparison. They haven't left it to the customer to subconsciously include other options in the internal comparison.

They also introduced something called a decoy price. They're not really expecting anyone to choose the $125 print-only version; there is no point, but it's there as a decoy to make the print plus online option look like fantastic value for money.

Comparisons can take many forms.

If a discount is offered, it makes sense to show a 'was' price to compare against. If the manufacturer has one, you can compare against an RRP.

Even better, it makes sense to have more than one product or solution in a category. If you are a manufacturer you might have a good/better/best set of options or trim levels.

If you are tendering to provide a service, you can usually identify options that a client might not have considered; that gives you the opportunity to offer two, or even better three different solutions at three different prices.

Chapter 9. Price Anchors

Price anchors are numbers that influence the price a customer is prepared to pay. They can be real (what customers are used to paying) or completely unrelated to the product, but they still influence the price.

A price anchor is a number that you have in your head that says "this is a reasonable price to pay" for something. For example, most people have a feeling for what is a reasonable price to pay for a gallon of petrol at the current time. If you drive past a garage where it is 10p or 20p more expensive than you're currently paying, then it looks expensive. But anchors do move over time, so if petrol is currently at £1.30 and the price of a barrel of crude oil drops, resulting in a drop of the pump price to £1.10, then that looks incredibly cheap until the anchor renormalises.

There is something very interesting about anchors. The anchor doesn't actually have to be anything real, it can be a completely arbitrary number that has been put in the customer's mind.

Horizon, a BBC science program, aired an episode looking at how people make decisions. They arranged for one of their team to walk along a river bank with a bottle of champagne in his hand, asking people how much they would be willing to pay for it. Before he asked them that question, however, he held out a bag which he said contained 100 ping pong balls numbered 0-99. He asked them to pick a ping pong ball out and tell him what the number is. Then he asked them how much they would pay for the bottle of champagne.

Of course, there weren't really 100 different ping pong balls. He had two bags, one full of 10s and one full of 65s.

The people who pulled a ping pong ball out of the 10 bag offered between £10 and £12. Those who pulled the ping pong ball out of the 65 bag offered between £40 and £60. So, just the arbitrary act of reading out a number created a temporary price anchor in their heads.

This can be used in a number of ways. The product name could include a number which could create an anchor; or before the price is mentioned the value the product or service creates (assuming it is bigger than the price!) could be discussed.

As well as being arbitrary, anchors can be real.

The order in which you present prices makes a difference. Imagine you are buying carpet and you needed underlay to go beneath it.

6mm PU Foam	9mm PU Foam	11mm PU Foam	11mm Sponge	9mm Crumb
£2.99	£4.99	£5.99	£7.99	£9.99

The shop has five different levels of underlay quality, and mounts them on a presentation board. Because we count up, our natural inclination is to present things in ascending order. So, per square metre, the prices would be presented as £2.99, £4.99, £5.99, £7.99 and £9.99 in that order.

What happens is that customers see the £2.99/m2 underlay first and anchor on that. They often don't go for the very cheapest, they think they can afford to spend a bit more for slightly better quality, and the most popular product then becomes the £4.99/m2.

But what happens if you simply reverse the order?

9mm Crumb	11mm Sponge	11mm PU Foam	9mm PU Foam	6mm PU Foam
£9.99	£7.99	£5.99	£4.99	£2.99

If the customer sees the £9.99/m2 option first then they anchor on it, particularly if they get a chance to experience the quality by putting it on the floor and walking on it. Even if the customer doesn't choose the £9.99/m2 underlay they will often choose the £7.99/m2 one instead.

The next thing you can do with anchors is break them.

There is a laptop brand called Alienware. It has an angular, sharp and futuristic design, reminiscent of a Lamborghini. When you switch it on, the power button is an alien's head, and an alien's face appears on the screen. All the keys light up with deep red colours, and the track pad is illuminated blue. Under the skin, it's a Dell laptop. Its performance is slightly better than the nearest equivalent to Dell but it costs 50% more, particularly when Dell first bought the brand.

What happens is that by creating a different experience, Dell are breaking the comparison against their standard, off-the-shelf products and gaining a premium price.

This is exactly what happened with Starbucks. In 1998, Starbucks entered the market and suddenly customers were no longer buying a simple cup of coffee; they were buying a coffee experience. The language changed - we now buy from a barista; the sizes are grande, venti, trente; the coffee is made using a machine which does interesting things, hisses steam and makes lots of noise. The whole experience changed. If anything, the service got worse - now it takes a lot longer to buy coffee than it ever used to.

The raw material cost hardly changed. The ingredients are slightly more expensive, but not 5 times more expensive. Yet we are paying a lot more for that experience, we went from paying £0.50 a cup to £2.50 a cup.

So there are three things you can do with anchors. You can create arbitrary anchors through either the naming of the product or something around the product - a number that just creates a temporary anchor. You can create an anchor through the order in which you create the products. Or you can break the anchor, so you're stopping that comparison from taking place.

Chapter 10. Pricing vs Value

The price of something communicates a lot about the quality and value of what you're going to receive, and therefore it can be a mistake to try too low a price because you're telling people that it's a low quality item. If you use a higher price, you're telling people it's a high quality items and high quality items often sell more.

In the early 2000s a mail order company called CPC ran a test.

CPC had around 80,000 customers, and once a month they mailed the most active 60,000 of those customers. CPC sold a lot of office equipment, computers, maintenance equipment and electronic components, and this particular mailshot focused on computer equipment.

The mailer had 64 pages. For the test, three versions of the outside cover were printed, so this affected the outside and inside, front and back pages - these are the most important selling pages. The price was increased for 20,000 of the mailings, decreased for 20,000, and kept the same as the previous months for 20,000.

What would you expect the outcome to be?

Economists would describe this as the price elasticity curve. The expected result would be that where you decrease the price of something the demand should go up, and where you increase the price the demand should go down.

What CPC actually observed was the sales volume of the most expensive items went up. The sales volume of the items with the price decrease also went up, but not as much. They sold more of the more expensive products compared to the two alternatives - no price change and a lower price.

Why? Well partly because price communicates something about the quality of what you are going to receive.

Back in the 80's and 90's, there was a saying - "no one ever got fired for buying IBM". This was at a time when IBM's competition was generally more innovative or superior in performance, and usually lower on price, and this covered everything from desktop PCs all the way up to mainframes.

Why did an IBM logo command a price premium?

It was because the buyer was taking the risk out of the purchase. That's what the saying means, after all. The buyer knew it was going to be a quality, reliable product that would not break down. In practice IBM was probably no more reliable than its main competitors, but this was a powerful perception and the desire to avoid a problem was incredibly influential.

At the time, the computers that companies were buying were running those companies. If the computer breaks down and the whole company grinds to a halt then someone's head is going to be on the block. Professional buyers, who sales people think are only motivated by price, are also concerned about not losing their jobs because they've bought a substandard product that stops the factory.

Conversely, a low price also says something about the product. As has been discussed already, too low a price and the customer thinks there must be something seriously wrong with the product or service.

This was neatly demonstrated in the UK when the government accidentally ran a pricing experiment. In 2004 the government introduced student fees for university education and capped those fees at £3,000 per year. Then in 2012 the cap for student fees was increased to £9,000 per year.

The government expected the newer universities with the less academic or less established courses would remain at £3,000 a year and there would be a range of fees all the way up to the world-renowned universities which would charge £9,000 a year. What actually happened was that almost every single university charged £9,000. Why? Well, the headlines at the time said it all "Universities are imposing £9,000 so they won't look like a cheap option and discourage students from going there."

Price communicates something about value. So try a higher price.

Chapter 11. Power of Zero

This is about using 'free' in an appropriate way. Even though both price relativity and price anchors involve a mental comparison between a range of prices, when 'free' is introduced it shortcuts that internal comparison mechanism and stops it from taking place. 'Free' elements help to promote your product.

We established, when discussing price relativity that customers will mentally compare your price. They either compare with a direct or indirect competitor, with a substitute for that product, or with something else they can spend their money on. This is also the case with price anchors, where the higher first price creates an anchor for later prices.

When zero, or free, is introduced into the equation, it breaks the internal, subconscious ability to make those comparisons.

For example, research was performed in America where people were offered a high quality chocolate for 15 cents (a Lindt), or a lower quality chocolate for 1 cent (a Hershey's Kiss). Three quarters of the people asked chose the 15 cent Lindt, versus one quarter choosing the 1 cent Hershey's Kiss.[2]

Until the researches knocked one cent off both prices.

Following this nearly three quarters of the people chose the Hershey's Kiss and just over a quarter of the people chose the Lindt. The proportions were

---

[2] Zero as a Special Price: The True Value of Free Products: Shampanier, Mazar, Ariely. Marketing Science, Vol. 26, No. 6, November-December 2007, pp. 742-757

completely reversed. When the Hershey's Kiss is free, the normal price comparison process changes.

So how might you use this?

Clearly, you don't apply 'free' to your core product. Do not give it away for nothing.

However, there are options that you can identify which your customers will value and which are easy to offer as a supplement to the core product, such as free delivery, free gift wrapping, free seaside view, free 'plant a tree to offset your carbon', free embroidered name, free first 6 months warranty, free first service - whatever it might be.

This comes back to identifying the things your customers value when making the purchase decision. What is motivating them to buy one product compared to another? If there are low cost items to you but high value options to the customer, then they are things you can offer for free. They are the things that make it difficult to do that mental price comparison. They make the product look more compelling, and make the customer think "Not only do I get that, but I get this, this, and this all for free. Wow. How can I resist?"

Chapter 12. Arbitrary Precision

The more precise the price the less likely it is to be negotiated; it looks to the customer that there must be a good reason for it to be the price it is.

It has long been understood that reducing a price by a penny or a cent, for example from £20.00 to £19.99, reduces the *perceived* price. The price now looks like a 'tens' number whereas previously it was a 'twenties' number. This works, but it's not the whole story.

In fact, the more precise **any** price is, the smaller it seems to the customer; and in addition, the more it looks like it has been arrived at through detailed and scientific analysis, and so the less likely they are to negotiate the price down.

One interesting piece of research[3] investigated how we (humans, that is) estimate the size or magnitude of a number. We do this estimation because we don't carry calculators around in our heads. Intuitively you can see that this is true - if you were handed a heavy object you probably couldn't say with any accuracy what the weight is in kilograms, but you can definitely say whether it's 'heavy' or 'light'. You can also easily compare the weight of one object with another. We're good at scaling things, we're very poor at determining an absolute value.

We do this with numbers too. It turns out that the more precise a number is, the smaller it 'feels' to us internally. As a consequence, when people are tested, £325,425 *feels* like a smaller number than exactly £325,000. Precise numbers, in our heads, feel smaller than they really are.

The next two pieces of research analysed real market data. The first looked at house sales[4]. 27,000 transactions in Florida were analysed where the original asking price was compared with the final sale price, and the fewer zeros in the original price the closer the final price was to that original asking price. Or, to put it another way, the more precise the original price the less negotiation took place.

In the second piece of research[5] exactly the same was found when company mergers and acquisitions were analysed. The more precise price the company was offered for sale the closer to that price was the final agreement. As has been said already, these psychological factors affect B2B sales as much as they do B2C sales.

It's not hard to unpack some of what's happening inside people's heads during negotiations like these. If a price is extremely round, such as £10,000 for a service you're going to provide or a product you want to sell, it feels to the customer as if you've just stuck your finger in the air and guessed a

[3] Manoj Thomas, Daniel H. Simon, Vrinda Kadiyali: 'Do Consumers Perceive Precise Prices to be Lower Than Round Prices? Evidence from Laboratory and Market Data', Johnson School Research Paper Series #09-07, 2007

[4] Malia F. Mason, Alice J. Lee, Elizabeth A. Wiley, Daniel R. Ames: 'Precise offers are potent anchors: Conciliatory counteroffers and attributions of knowledge in negotiations.' Journal of Experimental Social Psychology, 2013

[5] Petri Hukkanen, Matti Keloharju: 'Initial Offer Precision and M&A Outcomes', Aalto University, Harvard Business School, CEPR, and IFN, November 2, 2015

number. "Well", they will think (consciously or unconsciously), "if it's ok for you to guess then it's ok for me to guess too, and who's to say your guess is any better than mine?" So they will come back with a counter offer, "why don't we call it £6,000?"

Straightaway, you're into a negotiation for a deep discount and you will be lucky if you end up at £8,000. If your original asking price was £10,440 it will look like there's a rational reason for it and they are much less likely to start their negotiate with £6,000.

The key message, then, is to avoid rounding your price or quote. If your service or product would normally be priced at around £10,000, don't take a small amount off to make it more precise, add something on.

One advantage to having a precise price is that it makes future price increases easier. If you currently charge £100 for something then it is blindingly obvious to the customer when you increase your prices; if you currently charge £103 or even £104.99 then a price increase is less obvious.

By the way, a word of warning - you don't want to be **too** precise because (apart from some special circumstances) if you quote an amazingly precise number, such as £10,448.39, it starts to look strange. It would have to be a genuinely precise number that you could defend.

Chapter 13. Elective Pricing

Let the customer choose to pay what they think your product or service is worth.

Letting a customer choose whether they are going to pay you, and if so, how much they are going to pay you, sounds like a recipe for disaster.

In October 2007 Radiohead launched the album *In Rainbows*. For the first two months of release it was available for download, but they didn't put a price on it - they let the listener decide what they wanted to pay. On a per album basis, they made less money than they would if they had sold a CD through shops. But, because this was online and the distribution cost was effectively zero, and because they sold far more albums than they would have done through traditional channels, in total they actually made more money.

In Saltaire in West Yorkshire there is a small café that does not charge for its food at all. If you want, you can go in there and eat completely for free every single day and they will not mind. But they do ask you to consider paying what you think the meal was worth if you enjoyed the food, and they are thriving.

This has been done elsewhere. Other cafes have tried saying "this coffee is free, but typically a customer might pay £2.50 for it". What they find is that customers appreciate the quality of the food and the experience so much that they pay more than they probably would have done if they had been charged a fixed price for the food.

Pay-what-you-want has been tested in book publishing. The Data Science Handbook, by Shan, Wang, Chen and Song, compared a number of different models[6]. They had 5700 email subscribers who had expressed an interest in the book prior to publication, and they randomly divided them up into seven groups. The groups varied between two different fixed prices; two suggested prices with no minimum price so the customer could pay what they want; and three groups with a minimum price and a suggested price, but the customer could pay anything over the minimum.

When the book was launched and they analysed the data, the version with the maximum revenue was one where the minimum price was $20 but they suggested that most purchasers usually pay $29.

An area where pay-what-you-want often works well is the professional services market where the service is personally delivered and there is a strong relationship between the customer and the provider. There are examples where the average payment for services are higher than a normal fee would have been; your customers feel an emotional need to reward you for what they have received.

Another area where pay-what-you-want is used is as a negotiating tool. Imagine a scenario where you have used various pricing techniques to

---

[6] Shan, Wang, Chen, Song: "You Can Earn As Much Or More From A Pay-What-You-Want Model As From A Fixed Price Model", Forbes: May 29, 2015

position your price as positively as you can, but you are still coming under price pressure. Perhaps there are other competitors still in the running. At this point many companies simply give in and match the competitor's price in order to retain the business. However, an alternative approach would be to say that the customer is free to pay that minimum amount; most customers pay more because of the quality of the product/service, and you will leave it up to the customer to decide how much that will be. Some customers will just pay the minimum, but you are no worse off compared to what you were prepared to do anyway; some will pay extra, so on average you have made more money.

Chapter 14. Hyperbolic Discounting

Customers perceive a lower value for money in the future compared to now, and the value they perceive drops off rapidly - it follows a hyperbolic curve. This means that payments deferred into the future feel like smaller amounts than payments made now.

You can buy things now or in the future; for things you buy now you can pay now or in the future. The perceived price you have paid or are willing to pay is a curve that changes with time, and the curve is called a hyperbola. This is basically saying people value money much more now compared to some point in the future.

Therefore, if you are able to offer pricing where the payments are at some point in the future people are often prepared to pay more for the item, particularly if you are using this as a mechanism to upsell from one product to a superior (and more expensive) product.

Research[7] backs this up. If you ask somebody "which would you prefer, £100 right now or £120 in two weeks' time?", most people prefer the £100 pounds now. If you ask people "would you like £100 in 50 weeks or £120 in 52 weeks", which is effectively the same as the first option, most people choose £120 in 52 weeks.

---

[7] Redden, Joseph P. (2007), "Hyperbolic Discounting", in Encyclopedia of Social Psychology

The second option demonstrates that people genuinely understand that £120 is worth more than £100 and it is worth waiting two weeks extra. But the first option gives them the opportunity to have cash in hand immediately, and £100 right now feels more valuable than £120 in two weeks. After all, something might happen, the offer might be withdrawn.

The same effect occurs with options such as £50 now or £100 in the future, and with different options regarding when you can have each amount of money.

How do we apply this?

'Buy now, pay later' is an obvious concept which has been widely used.

You can also use it to drive sales towards higher value products to increase the average order value.

Imagine two products, Product A and Product B. Product B is superior in performance to Product A. Product A costs £700 (unless you have applied arbitrary precision!) and Product B is £900.

Many customers, comparing those two products, would probably choose the cheaper one if that would satisfy their needs. However, most would also desire the superior product if they could afford it. If you offer the £700 Product with payment now or the £900 Product but you don't pay for 6 months, the value of that money in the future feels lower than it really is. People are then more likely to upgrade to the more expensive product.

Chapter 15. Price Abstraction

The further away your prices are from being expressed in an actual currency, or the further away the transaction is from actual cash, the more people are prepared to pay for something.

The advent of credit cards in the 1950s/1960s was a massive boost for retail. Partly it was because consumers didn't have to save to buy something they wanted any more, they could get it now; but it was also because paying for something with a card just feels less painful than if you are pulling real cash out of a wallet or purse.

This is part of the reason why casinos use chips. Obviously, they don't want a lot of money on the gaming tables due to the security risk that would introduce, but there is another aspect. Unless you go to casinos a lot the face value of each chip is not immediately obvious; they are all the same size, and although they are colour coded you have to learn the colours. A £5 chip just doesn't look or feel like it is really £5. It's very easy to end up spending a lot more than you think.

Each step that takes you away from actual cash, the higher your propensity to spend more.

Companies offer financing facilities, or break a sale down into free financing and individual monthly payments. Both of those things start to move you away from the cash price.

This is perhaps why Getty Images price their images in points. An individual image might be 5 points, a high res version 10 points, or a super high resolution 15 points. You buy the points up front in a block, but when it comes to buying the image you have to do the mental arithmetic to convert the points into cash, and not only are our brains lazy and don't want the bother, even when they do, it still doesn't feel like a real cash value.

Another option to consider is to combine this with a customer loyalty programme. As the customer interacts with you they build up points which don't necessarily have a defined face value - you don't declare that points are worth 50p each or whatever. But the points can be redeemed for things that do have a value, such as service calls or upgrades. The customers accumulate something that has a value but they can't necessarily put a monetary price on it; however they would feel the loss if they were to move to a competitor.

A quick summary of the eight pricing concepts we have discussed.

Customers compare prices, either with competitor's products, alternatives or just something else they can spend the money on. Price relativity is all about giving them something to compare against. It also includes considering decoy prices to make the price of one option look like fabulous value for money.

A price anchor is a number you have in your head which guides what you are prepared to pay for something. Anchors can be real, they can be completely arbitrary (such as a model name), or can be simply based on the order in which prices are presented. If you can't create an anchor you can always try to break existing anchors.

A higher price indicates that the customer is going to receive higher value, and often leads to higher rather than lower sales - price vs value.

Making something free (not your main product or service) or giving something away disrupts the whole price comparison mechanism in the purchaser's mind.

Arbitrary precision makes a price sound scientifically calculated, and makes it less likely that negotiation will take place; and if it does, the discounts negotiated are smaller.

Sometimes you can let the customer decide what to pay - elective pricing. The customer pays what they think the product or service is worth. You can help guide that with minimum prices or messages such as "here is what other people have paid in the past".

People perceive a higher 'value' for money they have now compared to money in the future, so hyperbolic discounting would be a way to upsell to more expensive products which are paid for in the future.

Price abstraction is simply the concept that the further away from real hard cash your prices are expressed, the more the customer is willing to pay.

→ credit cards / casino chips.

Section 4 - Deciding on the Best Approach

You now have eight concepts, each of which can help you to effectively and successfully communicate a higher price to your customers in a way that makes it more likely they will accept that higher price. So which are you going to implement?

The first point to make is that you should not try to implement all, or even most, of them at the same time. Trying to make too many changes all at once is hard and often fails, and it makes it almost impossible to understand which concepts are working.

Step one, therefore, is to refer back to Chapter 6. Buyer Behaviour. Here you worked out where your specific market segment sits with regard to frequency of purchase and importance of purchase.

For Business to Consumer (B2C) markets....

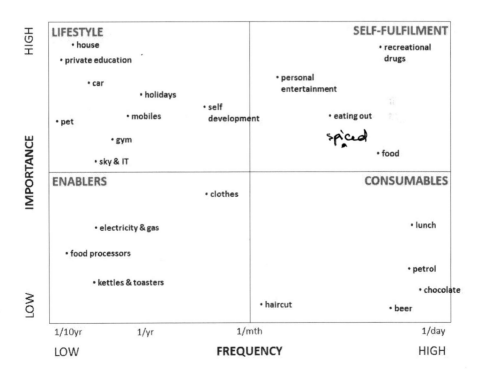

For Business to Business (B2B) markets…

	STRATEGIC			PRODUCTION
HIGH	• assets/plant			• key components
	• ERP s/w			
	• servers	• marketing	• minor plant	
			• health & safety	
	• telephony/ISP	• finance/factoring	• temp labour	
IMPORTANCE	• insurance	• HR		
	• accountants		• recruitment	• minor components
	ENABLERS			CONSUMABLES
	• utilities	• laptops/software		
		• furniture		
	• catering		• travel	
	• cleaners			• petrol
LOW			• copy paper • coffee/tea	• nuts & bolts

1/10yr	1/yr	1/mth	1/day
LOW		FREQUENCY	HIGH

Although, in principle, any concept can be applied in almost any circumstance, some are more appropriate than others for each quadrant of the Buyer Behaviour model. The map of which concepts work best in which quadrant is:

		FREQUENCY	

HIGH (IMPORTANCE)

STRATEGIC
- Price Relativity
- Price vs Value
- Price Anchors
- Hyperbolic Discounting
- Elective Pricing
- Arbitrary Precision

PRODUCTION
- Price vs Value ✓
- Price Anchors ✓
- Price Abstraction
- Arbitrary Precision ✓

ENABLERS
- Price Relativity
- The Power of 0
- Price vs Value
- Price Anchors
- Price Abstraction
- Hyperbolic Discounting
- Elective Pricing
- Arbitrary Precision

CONSUMABLES
- The Power of 0 ✓
- Price vs Value
- Price Anchors
- Price Abstraction
- Elective Pricing
- Arbitrary Precision

LOW (IMPORTANCE)

1/10yr	1/yr	1/mth	1/day
LOW		FREQUENCY	HIGH

Use this as a guide. If a concept looks like it applies to your situation - because every marketing situation faced by every company is slightly different - then by all means, test it.

One of the important things here is the word **test**. Anything you try out should be tested because you want to know two things - does it work, and if so, how *well* does it work. This is especially true for any change that is high-risk, which probably applies to any products or services that fall into either of the two high-importance quadrants.

Once you have decided which of the concepts you are going to implement, you need to work out *how* to implement them. What follows are some examples of how a concept might be applied. Every business, market and segment is different, so don't limit yourself to the ideas listed - use your imagination and think about your own circumstances.

The key point with regard to Price Relativity is that a customer always compares prices - against the competition, alternatives, substitutes, or just something else entirely on which they can spend their money.

The first step, therefore, is to make sure you have a range of products, solutions or offers that people can compare against each other. If you've only got one product in an area, is there anything you can do to create at least one, if not two alternatives - a good, better, best? If we refer back to the Economist example, they had two alternatives (online or print), and they introduced a third option by bundling the two together.

The next step is to refer back to the graph of price vs value that you developed in Chapter 5. Buyer Influences and Value Perception.

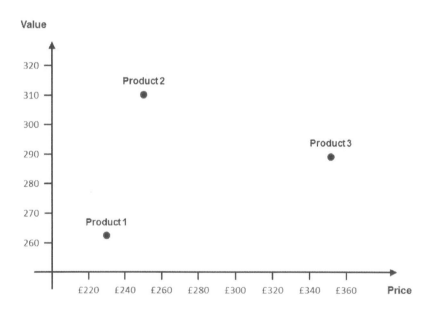

Typically, if you have three product alternatives in an area, you would expect to see three options almost in a straight line. The higher the price, the more value being delivered. In this example, that is not the case. This means there is an opportunity to reposition Product 2 by increasing its price.

You can use the price vs value graph to plan how you will position each product relative to each other. You can also look for opportunities to introduce a decoy price, where the price of one item is positioned specifically to make the product you want to sell look like excellent value for money.

There are other ways to introduce a comparison.

A common option when an item is on sale is to show the 'was' price, as in: Was £17.99, now £12.99. This is an obvious step, but not one that is always taken. A similar idea is to show an RRP, such as: RRP £5.99, our price £3.99.

Chapter 18. Price Anchors

There are a number of ways to introduce a price anchor.

As with Price Relativity, one step is to ensure there is more than one product option and to introduce those products starting with the highest priced item first.

For example, it may be that you provide a service of some kind such as web site development. Your customer comes to you with a specification, asking for a website to perform a specific function, and you prepare a quote. As an expert in web development, it would not be surprising if there were options over and above what is in the specification that would add value to the customer - that allows you to include a higher quote.

Without that higher quote, when the customer hears the actual quote they will immediately compare it with their internal expectation and with competing quotes; with the higher quote mentioned first, the customer anchors on this and compares the actual quote to that.

This works even better if, like Price Relativity, you can introduce more than two options to compare between.

Another way to create an anchor is through product naming. You typically sell your Gizmo for around £200, so calling it the Gizmo 300 creates a very temporary anchor.

An RRP is another obvious anchor. "Normally this product sells for £599, we're selling it for £499."

Listing the benefit the customer will experience similarly creates an anchor, and, even better, also demonstrates value for money. For example, perhaps you have a product which improves manufacturing efficiency by 5% and which you sell for £8,000. You're preparing a quote for a client, and you know their annual manufacturing costs are £500,000. In that case a 5% saving is worth £25,000, so discussing this first creates an anchor.

If creating an anchor is a challenge then you can look for mechanisms to break anchors - ways to differentiate your product or service from the competition by changing the vocabulary around the product, the environment where the product or service is consumed, the packaging, or anything else that changes the customer experience. Don't forget Starbucks!

Chapter 19. Pricing vs Value

This is relatively simple to implement - just try a higher price!

Of course, there is a bit more to it than that.

The key tool is the one where you worked out the Price Potential for your product or service, given an analysis of the break-even cost (based on simplified ABC), the minimum credible price, and the maximum realistic price.

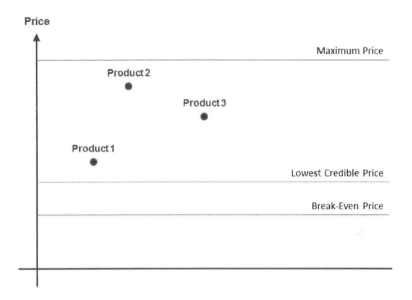

If your product/service is not at the top of the band but, when you compare the value of your product/service to your competition, you have a competitive advantage then you need to be brave enough to price your product appropriately.

Price increases can be used to smooth demand. If you are approaching capacity then try increasing prices to reduce demand. Of course, it is entirely possible that the higher price might communicate higher quality and value which actually increases demand, but as they say - that would be a nice problem to have!

Chapter 20. Power of Zero

Offering options for free helps to stop price comparisons from taking place, and make whatever you are selling look like great value.

Critical Sales Factor	Weighting	Product 1		Product 2		Product 3	
		Score	Total	Score	Total	Score	Total
Specification	9	8	72	10	90	10	90
Quality	10	6	60	8	80	10	100
30 day terms	4	10	40	10	40	10	40
Price	6	6	36	5	30	3	18
Availability	10	9	90	10	100	6	60
Total			298		340		308

But what to offer for free? In Chapter 5. Buyer Influences and Value Perception we developed the table above, which shows us what elements constitute 'value' from the point of view of the customer and how they rank those value items.

First, work out what it costs to deliver each of the Critical Sales Factors that constitute value. Map each CSF on a chart where the axis are value, low to high, and price, low to high. You are looking for options with a perceived high value with a low implementation cost - these are the elements that you can offer for free.

If there are no obvious CSFs that you can separate out as a distinctly priced item which can be offered as 'free', then you can think through all the other things that your customer might value. These are things that are not critical to the sale, but which are still valued - such as free delivery, free gift wrapping, free name engraving, free sea view, free seat upgrade, free drink and popcorn, or anything else. Plot these on the same chart of value vs price to see which ones are the cheapest to offer but are valued the most by your customers.

You can also use 'free' to smooth demand. For example, perhaps you run a hotel. In the off season you might offer the river room or a sea view as a free upgrade to your most regular customers. You're offering something for free which is actually costing you nothing because those superior rooms would be unoccupied anyway.

Chapter 21. Arbitrary Precision

This is another simple concept to implement.

The starting point is to list your current prices for your products; or, if this is a brand new product, what the potential price is. You then **add** an arbitrary amount - for example, if you normally sell something for £500 then try selling it for £532.

Let's take two examples.

If something is a physical product, such as selling curtains online, there is nothing to stop you from pricing a specific curtain at £129.11. You can justify the price based on the material costs and the effort to make the curtains.

If you provide a service such as website design, and you would normally charge £5,000 for a specific level of functionality and complexity, you could charge £5,190. Or perhaps you work on an hourly rate and charge £50 per hour, in which case you could charge £53 per hour.

When you create the arbitrarily precise price you will normally go up in price, not down.

However, don't be too precise if doing so would make the price look strange.

Quoting £5,192.19 for the website will seem slightly peculiar. The exception to this would be if you can quantify the reason for the extreme precision. Perhaps you have a formula in a spreadsheet which breaks each step down to its actual cost and you simply multiply each by the time estimated to complete it. In that case you will be able to justify the precision.

Chapter 22. Price Abstraction

The further away from cash a transaction is the easier it is to charge more - the price feels less real and more abstract.

A typical solution is to investigate finance options, the 'buy now, pay later' model.

Even better, you can consider something that is not directly related to a cash price at all. For example, a customer could earn loyalty points or something similar each time they interact with you, which are then redeemed in the future for something the customer values. Perhaps the next upgrade costs £348 or 2,850 loyalty points - so what is a point worth? It's a difficult mental computation and it makes the points feel really valuable.

Another option is to actually sell blocks of points. Getty Images, who own iStock Photo, use this method. They sell blocks of points which they call 'credits', and the user exchanges these credits when they decide they need an image.

This does three things. First, the credits are bought at one point in time and the image is downloaded at a later point, so the transaction has been separated in time from the sale. Second, it's hard to work out what an image really costs if it is expressed in points. Third, the 'size' of the points (e.g. an image is 3 points) would normally be smaller than the numbers in the real price (e.g. those 3 points are equivalent to £4.50), so the '3' creates a smaller anchor.

Chapter 23. Elective Pricing

Sometimes giving people the choice of what to pay can either increase the average order value or can dramatically increase sales volumes.

Whether you are going to try this will depend on a number of factors.

First, you need to consider what your unit cost is. If it is close to zero (for example, music downloads) then a high demand which is not balanced by a high average order value will not cause problems by creating a major cost burden.

Second, you should think about how you can run tests which are isolated from the rest of your transactions. For example, if you provide a service to clients, you can easily decide to test Elective Pricing with your next three clients without affecting your relationship with your other clients and without committing you to Elective Pricing for all future work.

So how do you go about implementing or testing this?

First, decide whether you are going to allow the customer or client to decide what price to pay without any guidance, whether you are going to have a suggested price, or whether you are going to have a minimum price.

Then, decide how you are going to run tests. You might do it by geography (offering Elective Pricing to customers in one location that you can compare to other locations), by date (try it for a month then compare to previous months), or if you don't have repeat customers then you can simply randomly choose which customers to offer it to. If you sell at a distance, perhaps from a website, then you can offer Elective Pricing randomly (perhaps based on whether there is an odd or even number of letters in their surname!).

Chapter 24. Hyperbolic Discounting

In essence, hyperbolic discounting is the human tendency to prefer smaller payoffs now over larger payoffs later, because people discount the value of money in the future.

The most common way to use this concept is with financing, such as 'buy now pay later':

In fact, any system which puts payment off into the future, such as credit cards or a PayPal account, uses the same concept.

The technique can also be used to upsell. Let's say you have two products, A and B. A is priced at £535, and B is priced at £874. B is clearly superior in performance and value to A, this is recognised by your customers, and B is the more desirable product.

Given a free choice, all customers would rather have product B. Most people buy product A, though, because they are price conscious.

What you can do is offer product A at £535 but you pay now, or product B at £874 *but you pay in 6 months or 12 months*. To do this you need to be able to finance this delayed payment yourself or, much more likely, to have financing in place. That financing will cost money, and you either need to have enough margin in product B to cover those costs or you need to slightly increase the price of product B to cover the financing costs.

Chapter 25. Planning Potential Upside or Downside

You have considered which concepts you're going to try and thought about how to implement them. Now we need to look at what the overall impact of the pricing test is going to be.

There are three possible sales outcomes from any test, and they are fairly obvious - sales go down, sales stay the same, or sales go up. However, if sales go down does that mean that the test of any pricing concept has been a failure? Not necessarily.

If your net margins have increased because of the price increase, then you can afford to lose some sales and either make the same profit or actually make more profit. For example, if you normally make a 10% net margin and you increase your prices by 5% then your net profit will now be close to 15%. If you lose 20% of your previous sales volume then you are actually better off!

The following chart illustrates this. It shows how much sales can decline following a price increase and still make the same amount of actual profit.

		Current Net Profit				
		5%	**10%**	**15%**	**20%**	**25%**
Price Increase	**3%**	-38%	-23.1%	-17%	-13%	-11%
	6%	-55%	-38%	-29%	-23%	-19%
	9%	-64%	-47%	-38%	-31%	-26%
	12%	-71%	-55%	-44%	-38%	-32%
	15%	-75%	-60%	-50%	-43%	-38%

Let's do a simple calculation to illustrate this. Imagine your turnover is £1million, then at 10% net profit you make £100k each year. If you increase your prices by 3% then your net margin increases to 13%. If sales decline by 23% then you are now turning over £770k, and 13% of £770k is still £100k.

The real point is that any decline in sales *less* than 23% would mean that you are actually making more total £ profit.

Having gone through the simplified activity-based costing process you will have a good understanding of your net margin for each product, product group or market segment. You can use this net margin to check what sales decline you can afford in the chart above.

If sales do reduce but you are still making the same profit then you're not working as hard for the same amount of money. That means you have additional time and resources to put into growing your company.

You're now ready to go ahead and test it all out.

Section 5 - Measurement

You want to know what works and what doesn't. That means that when you do your tests, how you measure the outcomes is critical.

There are two prime methods of testing - A/B testing and longitudinal testing.

A/B testing is where you set up a minimum of two scenarios which are running simultaneously. This is the gold standard of testing because one scenario is normally exactly what you were doing before, and this is the control group - let's call that the 'A' group. It's the baseline that you will compare against. The second scenario is what you are testing - call that the 'B' group.

If there is more than one concept you are testing you have A, B, and C groups. You split your customers into groups of equal sizes which are equally representative of the customers as a whole. The only difference is the price they experience.

Imagine that you sell online. You could separate customers by geography and do a test where everybody in the north gets a new price and everybody in the south gets the price you have historically used. The danger is that it is easy to imagine differences in buyer behaviour between those two groups. Similarly, splitting customers by age, gender, incomes or occupation could all bias the results because the different groups will act differently.

A better way is either for the website to randomly provide option A to one customer and option B to a different customer, or alternate between the two options, or if that is difficult, to find something that is not linked to different customer behaviour. The first letter of their surname ought to be a completely random element, so you could test option A with the 'A to M' group and option B with the 'N to Z' group.

Find a way to randomly split your customers up and then run two or three different scenarios on those customers. The important thing is to do everything you can to end up with a test where the only variation is the price. At the end of the testing, compare the results.

The second type of testing is called longitudinal testing, and it is an alternative when it is not easy to do A/B testing. Let's imagine you have a coffee shop and you want to test Elective Pricing compared to your normal fixed price. It's very difficult to randomly pick out customers in the line and let some choose what they want to pay while the person next to them is charged £2.50.

Instead you split the test by time. You might, for a month, run a test where a cup of coffee is £2.00. This is your normal price, and all you do is count how many people come in and buy a cup of coffee during that period. You then run the test for a month at £2.50, again counting how many cups of coffee you sell. Next, for a month you tell the customer "Just pay whatever you think it is worth" and you count the total number of coffees sold and the total income. Finally, for a month you run the test where you say to customers "The coffee is normally £2.50 but just pay what you think it's worth", again counting how many cups of coffee are sold and the total revenue.

Now you can analyse the results. What you're looking for in the third and fourth months is not just what the average price was for the cup of coffee, but how many cups of coffee you sold. It may be that in the third month the average price that people paid was £1.90, so you're making less per cup of coffee - but if you sold twice as many cups of coffee then the total net profit might be much higher.

The disadvantage of a longitudinal test is that different months might have different sales anyway, perhaps due to seasonal influences. Although it takes longer, a way to check this is to repeat the sequence of tests. If you need to get to a result quicker than running each test for a month then you can run each for a week, as long as there are enough transactions in a week to give you confidence in the result.

However, there are two areas with regard to testing where you have to be careful.

It is one thing to run a specific A/B test for a limited time until you have gathered enough information to make a decision; it is another to charge different customers different prices over a longer period, where you run the risk of upsetting those customers who got charged the higher price, or to end up charging the same customer different prices on different days (if you are segmenting randomly). You need to plan and control things so that you do not displease customers.

With regard to running a longitudinal test, you need to be able to explain to repeat customers why they were paying one price on one day and then a different price on another day.

You must also be careful not to imply that a lower price might be a sale item unless you are complying with the specific legislation for your country. For example, in the UK, an item on sale must have been sold at the higher price for 28 consecutive days immediately before the sale, unless a sign explains the terms of the offer; you can't have something on sale for longer than it was offered at the higher price, unless you display a sign explaining why (such as something is being discontinued); and the original price must be clearly displayed along with the sale price. If you do all these things then you are no longer comparing one pricing concept with another, you are comparing your normal price with a sale price.

Conclusion

The challenge now is to be brave, to be creative, to think through the options and to try some out. Be prepared to put in a little bit of effort to figure out exactly where you are in terms of costs and current pricing, and consider which options might work best.

What are the platypuses in your business? Which pricing problems do you want to solve? Find those platypuses and put a price on their heads!

Once you have done that then it's over to you. Have a go, and good luck.

07702039572

Printed in Great Britain
by Amazon